acier National Park

An ABC Adventure

A hoary marmot checks out a visitor to Glacier National Park.

Glacier National Park
An A B C Adventure

KC GLASTETTER and JEREMIE HOLLMAN

Mountain Press Publishing Company
Missoula, Montana
2008

All photos by the authors

Front cover photo: Highline Trail, Logan Pass by Jeremie Hollman
Back cover photo: Lake McDonald by KC Glastetter

Library of Congress Cataloging-in-Publication Data

Glastetter, KC.
    Glacier National Park : an ABC Adventure / KC Glastetter and Jeremie Hollman. — 1st ed.
       p. cm.
    ISBN 978-0-87842-552-5 (pbk. : alk. paper)
    1. Glacier National Park (Mont.)—Juvenile literature. 2. English language—Alphabet—
Juvenile literature. 3. Alphabet books—Juvenile literature. I. Hollman, Jeremie. II. Title.
    F737.G5G53 2008
    978.6′52—dc22

2008034331

Printed in Canada by Friesens

Mountain Press Publishing Company
P.O. Box 2399
Missoula, Montana 59806

I dedicate this to my boys, who have taught me how to look at the world with a new set of eyes all over again.

—JH

Thanks to the "Glacier Girls" for all of the laughs and companionship on all of our many Glacier adventures.

—KCG

ACKNOWLEDGMENTS

Special thanks to Grant and Shannon for your support and hard work in helping make this book what it is. Thank you to Kelly Roth at the Glacier Institute for all of her help and assistance. Last but not least, thank you to Glacier National Park and its majestic beauty; without it, this book would not be possible.

GLACIER NATIONAL PARK

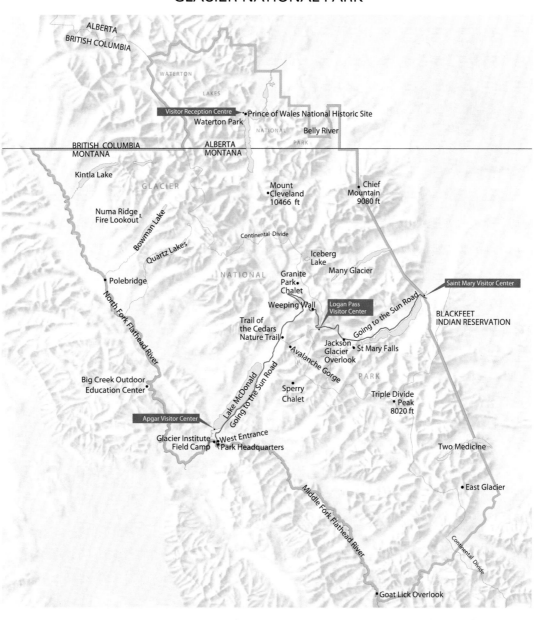

ALBERTA
BRITISH COLUMBIA

WATERTON

LAKES

NATIONAL

PARK

Visitor Reception Centre
Prince of Wales National Historic Site
Waterton Park
Belly River

BRITISH COLUMBIA
MONTANA

ALBERTA
MONTANA

Kintla Lake

GLACIER

Mount
Cleveland
10466 ft

Chief
Mountain
9080 ft

Numa Ridge
Fire Lookout

Bowman Lake

Continental Divide

Quartz Lakes

Iceberg
Lake

NATIONAL

Many Glacier

Polebridge

Granite
Park
Chalet

Saint Mary Visitor Center

Weeping Wall

Logan Pass
Visitor Center

Going to the Sun Road

BLACKFEET
INDIAN RESERVATION

North Fork Flathead River

Trail of
the Cedars
Nature Trail

Jackson
Glacier
Overlook

St Mary Falls

Avalanche Gorge

Big Creek Outdoor
Education Center

Lake McDonald

Going to the Sun Road

Sperry
Chalet

PARK

Triple Divide
Peak
8020 ft

Apgar Visitor Center

Glacier Institute
Field Camp

West Entrance
Park Headquarters

Two Medicine

East Glacier

Middle Fork Flathead River

Continental Divide

Goat Lick Overlook

A is for APGAR

Apgar is Glacier's west entrance. With lake access, shops, camping, and lodging, Apgar is the perfect place to start your journey into Glacier National Park. Take the Apgar Lookout Trail for an amazing view of Lake McDonald below.

A is for AVALANCHE GORGE

This gorge is formed by Avalanche Creek. The gorge is a steep, narrow canyon with waterfalls and rocky, moss-covered walls. The power of water continues to form and change the appearance of this gorge.

Bb

B *is for* BEAR GRASS

Bear grass is a tall stalked plant with a white cluster of flowers. Despite its name, bears don't eat it, and it's not really a grass. You might see deer and mountain goats munching on this lily cousin, and bears sometimes use it to soften up their dens for the winter. It is traditionally used by Native Americans to weave into baskets.

B *is for* BLACK BEAR

The black bear is Glacier's most abundant bear. This bear has round ears and is not always black. Unlike its cousin the grizzly, this bear shows no signs of a shoulder hump.

Cc

C *is for* CHIEF MOUNTAIN

This is one of the most prominent landmarks on the east side of Glacier Park. Located in the Lewis Range, it is a sacred place to many Native Americans.

C *is for* CEDAR

Abundant rain along the Continental Divide allows a lush oasis to thrive in the middle of the dry Rocky Mountains. The Trail of the Cedars leads through a forest of cedar, hemlock, cottonwood, and Douglas-fir where some trees are 500 years old and so immense that you can fit inside their trunks.

Dd

D *is for* DEER

There's a really good chance you will spot a deer. If you see big ears it's a mule deer; if you see a big white tail raised like a flag, you have found a white-tailed deer.

D *is for* DOUGLAS-FIR

One of Glacier's most common trees, the Douglas-fir is an evergreen, so it keeps its soft, flat, sweet-smelling needles all year long. Its seeds and dense foliage provide food and shelter for birds, squirrels, deer, and other animals.

Ee

E *is for* **ELK**

Male elk have impressive antlers. Elk have large brown bodies with darker necks and lighter rumps. Of all Glacier's hoofed mammals, elk are second only to the heftier moose in size.

E *is for* **EWE**

Ewes are Glacier's wild female bighorn sheep. You can tell the difference between males and females by the horns; ewes have small, slender horns, while rams have the huge curling horns that give the sheep its name. If you want to spot a ewe, keep your eyes open while hiking in Many Glacier.

Ff

F *is for* FIRE

Fire may seem scary and destructive, but it is a natural part of the Glacier ecosystem. Although it makes the ground look burnt and sooty, many plants and animals thrive after a fire, and soon a burned area will be green and teeming with life.

F *is for* FOX

This sly mammal has red fur and a large bushy tail. A relative of dogs and wolves, the red fox moves incredibly swiftly as it roams through Glacier, always on the hunt for berries, insects, mice, and voles.

Gg

G *is for* **GOING-TO-THE-SUN ROAD**

One of the world's most scenic drives, this 52-mile journey over the Continental Divide makes you feel like you are driving in a postcard. Construction was completed in 1932, and Going-to-the-Sun Road is now a National Historic Landmark.

G *is for* **GRIZZLY**

This is the animal, with a big shoulder hump, for which Glacier is best known. These large brown bears can grow up to be over 1,000 pounds! They may look like fierce hunters, but often the meat they eat is from animals that are already dead; most of their diet consists of berries, seeds, roots, and insects.

Hh

H *is for* **HUCKLEBERRY**

This dark purple berry grows on shrubs and has long been a staple for Native peoples. A favorite among hikers and bears, this tasty treat will burst in your mouth with tangy sweetness.

H *is for* **HARLEQUIN**

A duck that is fond of fast-flowing streams, the Harlequin migrates to Glacier in the spring. If you see a small, dark duck with white markings and a multicolored head, you may have spotted one.

Ii

I *is for* **INDIAN PAINTBRUSH**

The flower spike of Indian Paintbrush looks like it's been dipped in bright paint. The flowers are usually red, but can be orange, pink, or yellow. A meadow full of Indian paintbrush in full bloom is a picturesque sight.

I *is for* **ICEBERG LAKE**

Surrounded by mountains, this lake is often seen with bits of floating ice. On a hot summer's day you may be tempted to jump in and have a swim. But be prepared—the coldness of the water will shock you!

Jj

J *is for* JAMMER

These charming and historic red buses have been giving Glacier visitors a pretty sweet ride since the 1930s. The name "jammer" dates to the time before automatic transmissions when the drivers jammed the gears going up and down the steep roads.

J *is for* JACKSON OVERLOOK

This overlook is on Going-to-the-Sun Road, so you can get a good look at a glacier without a long hike. Jackson Glacier is one of the biggest glaciers in the park. Roadside signs will help explain what you see.

Shrinking Glaciers

 Kk

K *is for* **KIDS**

Are you a kid? Baby mountain goats are called kids, too. Whether you're a human or a goat, Glacier National Park is a wonderful place to be—there's no other place like it on Earth.

K *is for* **KINTLA LAKE**

This lake is quite beautiful and very remote. If you're looking for peace and quiet far from the crowds, Kintla Lake is a great place to hike, camp, kayak, or fish.

Ll

L *is for* **LOGAN PASS**
At the top of the Going-to-the-Sun
Road is Logan Pass, which marks
the Continental Divide. A boardwalk
will lead you past an abundance of
wildlife and wildflowers in summer.

L *is for* **LAKE MCDONALD**
This is the biggest of all Glacier's
lakes. It's ten miles long with a lodge
that has been famous since the early
1900s. If you get a chance, enjoy a
boat tour and soak up the beauty.

Mm

M *is for* **MOUNT CLEVELAND**

This is Glacier's highest peak; it towers above at 10,466 feet! Mount Cleveland is found near Glacier's northern border. Just below its north face, at the southern end of Waterton Lake, you can catch a boat and cruise into Canada's Waterton Lakes National Park.

M *is for* **MOUNTAIN GOATS**

With their special hooves, mountain goats can climb mountains and cliffs that would be impossible for most animals. Look way up high to spot their creamy white hair and black horns, and don't forget the binoculars!

Nn

N *is for* **NUMA RIDGE FIRE LOOKOUT**

The lookout ranger sits in this tower way up high and watches carefully for smoke and fires. You can hike to this lookout for amazing views of the surrounding mountains and Bowman Lake below.

N *is for* **NORTH FORK**

The North Fork of the Flathead River helps form the park's western boundary. Glacial runoff makes the water a gorgeous green, and it's a great place for floating and fishing.

Oo

O *is for* OWLS

Glacier is home to many species of owls, including great grays, great horned, and barred, as well as the northern hawk owl pictured here. The "hawk" in its name comes both from its appearance and from the fact that it hunts by day, like a hawk, and also at night, like most owls. Its hearing is so good that even rodents under snow are potential prey.

O *is for* OSPREY

This fish-eating raptor is mostly white with dark markings when seen from below. Ospreys nest on top of trees and poles near water. They're not shy, so if you're lucky you may get to see one swoop down and catch a fish.

Pp

P *is for* POLEBRIDGE

A tiny town found just outside Glacier's northwest border, this little place is surrounded by fantastic views. There are cabins for rent and a mercantile with the yummiest bakery goods to fuel your adventures in the park.

P *is for* PIKA

The pika is a small cold-climate creature that lives in burrows on rocky slopes. It looks like a hamster but is more closely related to rabbits. It is known for the squeaking alarm call it utters if it senses there's danger around.

Qq

Q *is for* QUARTZ LAKE

This lake has three parts: upper, middle, and lower. The upper lake is the biggest of the three. The Quartz Lake Loop trail is a beauty, and on it you'll also get to see Bowman Lake.

Q *is for* QUIET

The "Crown of the Continent" is known for its tranquility. Back in the woods where there's no one around, enjoy nature's peace and quiet. The wilderness that surrounds you in Glacier will set you aglow.

Rr

R *is for* **RIVER**

Over 900 miles of rivers and streams flow through Glacier. The park is home to the headwaters of three of North America's major rivers: the Columbia, the Missouri, and the Saskatchewan. You may want to enjoy the cool rush of their pristine waters by fishing, taking a rafting trip, or just admiring their beauty.

R *is for* **RAFTING**

Thrashing through whitewater in a man-made boat, it's human versus nature. Rafting is a fun and exciting outdoor activity. Glacier's rivers can be some of the wildest rides around. Many rafting guides are available to ensure that you safely enjoy your float down the rivers.

Ss

S *is for* SNOW

A winter in Glacier is full of this stuff and leads to fun explorations. Snow livens up mountains and is great for sightseeing and skiing. Due to the abundance of snow, many roads and trails, including Logan Pass, are closed for all but a few months a year.

S *is for* ST. MARY FALLS

These fifty-foot falls come down in two tiers. The clear blue waterfalls flow through cherry-colored rocks, serenading visitors with their sweet melodies.

Tt

T *is for* TRIPLE DIVIDE

Triple Divide Peak is where the Continental Divide meets the Northern Divide. Water here will flow one of three directions—west to the Pacific Ocean, east to the Atlantic Ocean, or north to Hudson Bay and the Arctic Ocean. This water flow marvel is quite amazing.

T *is for* TRAILS

These paths are for hiking, horseback riding, and having fun. They lead you to places that you're sure to like. Any way you travel, you'll love the more than 700 miles of trails in Glacier.

Uu

U *is for* **UPPER MCDONALD CREEK**
Spectacular views, falls, and aquamarine water await you along this creek. Harlequin ducks play in it during the early spring. Lookout platforms, bridges, and boardwalks provide easy access to some of the cleanest water in North America.

U *is for* **UNGULATE**
A hoof is really an enlarged toenail. Any mammal that has hooves is known as an ungulate. Moose, elk, deer, bighorn sheep, and mountain goats are the ungulates that call Glacier home.

Vv

V *is for* VELVET

Velvet is the soft, fuzzy skin that covers deer and elk antlers as they regrow each year. When the antlers are done growing the velvet dries up and starts to fall off. Sometimes you can find places on trees where a buck has rubbed his antlers to take the velvet off.

V *is for* VISITOR CENTER

There are four visitor centers within the park: Apgar, Logan Pass, St. Mary, and Waterton. Glacier Park rangers will help you learn all about the best hikes, places to camp, and how to get there, along with numerous facts about wilderness and wildlife.

Ww

W *is for* **WESTERN LARCH**

These tall native trees stand up high and proud. Even though they have cones and look like evergreens, they are deciduous. In the fall their needles turn bright yellow, setting gullies and hillsides ablaze with color before the needles fall off. The needles can be used to make a soothing tea.

W *is for* **WEEPING WALL**

Who knew rocks could cry? Weeping Wall near Logan Pass is a large wall of rock from which water seeps. It's fun to watch, and if you get in too close you may wind up soaked.

X is for XYLEM

How do plants and trees get a drink? There is a special tissue that carries water and minerals to the various parts of the tree or plant. This tissue is known as xylem. On a tree xylem is the woody part inside.

X is for X-COUNTRY SKIING

In winter when the roads are blocked with snow, what better way to enjoy the scenery than to strap on the planks? The park has many great routes for this winter activity where you can have an entertaining adventure and get a great workout.

← OUTER BARK

← PHLOEM

HEARTWOOD

← XYLEM

54

Yy

Y *is for* **YOU**

You are what this book is all about,
and you'll love going to Glacier!
You'll never truly know Glacier until
you've been there.

Y *is for* **YELLOW**

Fields of yellow glacier lilies in early
summer can make the park look like
a shower has rained down with gold.
Their eye-capturing beauty is quite
the sight to see.

56

Zz

Z *is for* ZIGZAG

Back and forth goes the trail up the mountain. All these side-to-side turns help you climb more easily. Zigzag trails, also known as switchbacks, can usually be found where the trail is the steepest.

Z *is for* ZILLIONS

There are countless and zillions of reasons to visit. You'll find being in Glacier really is incomparable. We hope this book was a fun Glacier expedition!

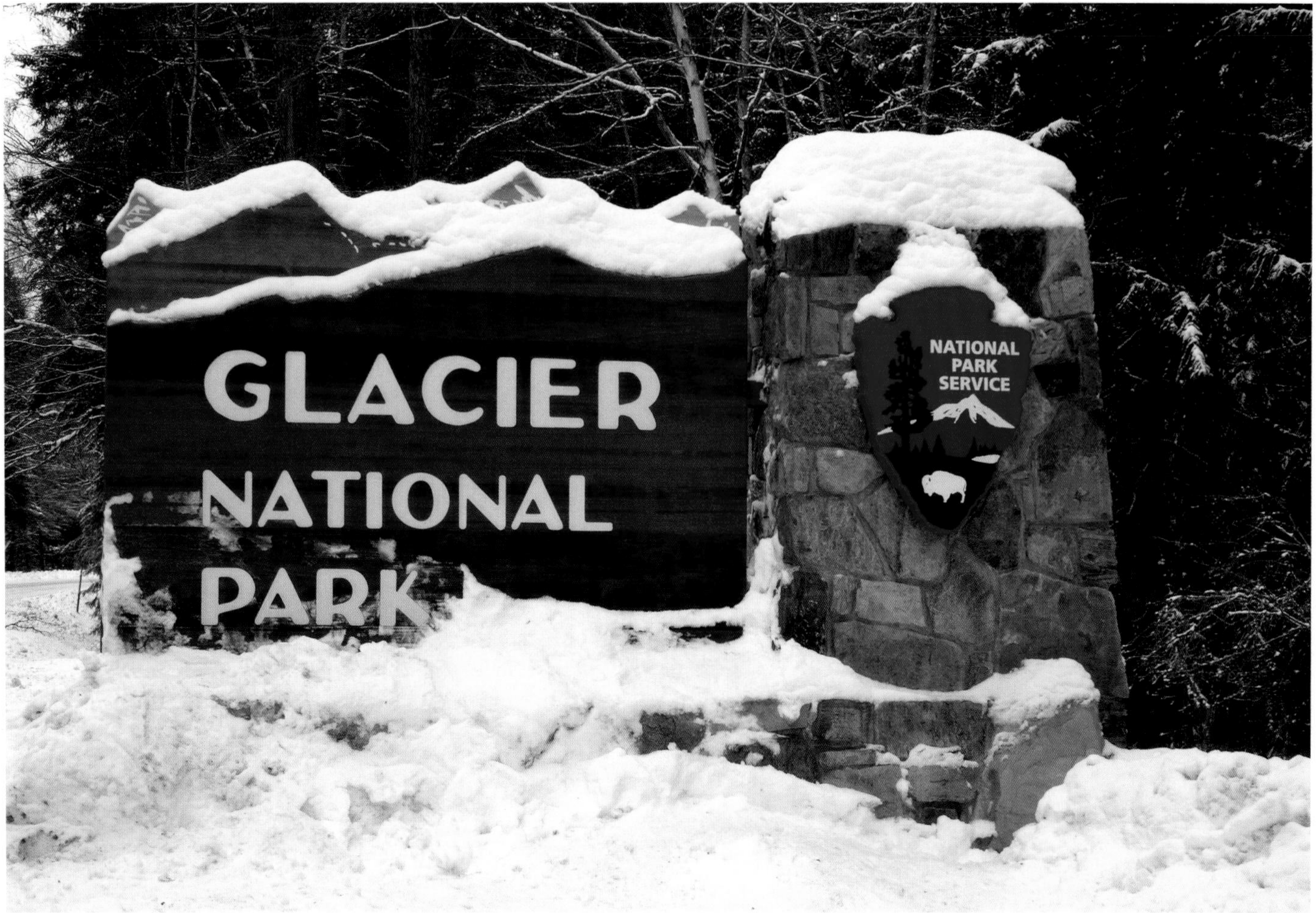
GLACIER
NATIONAL
PARK
NATIONAL
PARK
SERVICE

SUGGESTED RESOURCES

Web Sites:

www.nps.gov/glac
Official site of Glacier National Park.

www.nps.gov/learn/juniorranger.htm
Learn how to become a junior ranger in a national park.

www.glacierinstitute.org
Excellent field classes and camps for all ages.

www.glacierparkinc.com
Book a hotel room, jammer bus ride, or boat tour in the park.

www.glacierassociation.org
Visit the online bookstore of the Glacier National History Association.

www.montanaexposures.com
A collection of Montana photographs by the authors.

Books:

Best Easy Day Hikes: Glacier and Waterton Lakes. Erik Molvar. Guilford, CT: Falcon, 2007.
Great information on some of the parks' most popular hikes.

Animal Tracks of Glacier National Park. David S. Shea. West Glacier, MT: Glacier Natural History Association, 1986.
A must for identifying any tracks you might see in Glacier.

Plants of the Rocky Mountains. Linda Kershaw, Andy MacKinnon, and Jim Pojar. Edmonton, AB, Canada: Lone Pine Publishing, 1998.
An in-depth look at the flowers, grasses, and trees you might see in the Glacier area.

Smithsonian Handbooks: Birds of North America, Western Region. Fred J. Alsop III. New York: DK Publishing, 2001.
If you see a bird in Glacier, learn more about it with this field guide.

National Audubon Society Field Guide to Mammals. New York: Alfred A. Knopf, 1996.
Find out more about any mammal you might find in Glacier.

ABOUT THE AUTHORS

SHANNON HOLLMAN PHOTO

Jeremie Hollman is an avid fly fisherman and has tremendous love for wildlife. He embraces every opportunity given to him to be outdoors. Whether hiking, fishing, or just exploring, he always has his camera by his side and a picture to take home to tell a story of his adventures. Jeremie has a bachelor's degree in art from Fort Lewis College in Durango, Colorado. His writing and photographs have appeared in many state, regional, and national publications, as well as newspapers and calendars.

SHANNON HOLLMAN PHOTO

KC Glastetter has been an elementary school teacher for over twenty years and a photographer for five. She currently teaches third grade in Kalispell, Montana. KC and her family spend countless hours each year riding their tandem bicycle, hiking, cross-country skiing, and snowshoeing throughout the magnificent northwest. KC feels fortunate just to be outside in such incredible surroundings, and if she's lucky enough to capture a photograph, she is even richer for the experience.

Mountain Press Books for Young Readers

_____ *Awesome Ospreys: Fishing Birds of the World*, AGES 8 AND UP — $12.00

_____ *The Charcoal Forest: How Fire Helps Animals and Plants*, AGES 8 AND UP — $12.00

_____ *Loons: Diving Birds of the North*, AGES 8 AND UP — $12.00

_____ *Nature's Yucky!: Gross Stuff That Helps Nature Work*, AGES 5 AND UP — $10.00

_____ *Nature's Yucky! 2: The Desert Southwest*, AGES 5 AND UP — $12.00

_____ *Owls: Whoo are they?*, AGES 8 AND UP — $12.00

_____ *Sacagawea's Son: The Life of Jean Baptiste Charbonneau*, AGES 10 AND UP — $10.00

_____ *Snowy Owls: Whoo are they?*, AGES 8 AND UP — $12.00

_____ *Spotted Bear: A Rocky Mountain Folktale*, AGES 5 AND UP — $15.00

_____ *Stories of Young Pioneers: In Their Own Words*, AGES 10 AND UP — $14.00

Please include $3.00 shipping and handling for 1–4 books and $5.00 for 5 or more books.

Send the books marked above. I have enclosed $_____

Name _____ Phone_____

Address _____

City / State / Zip _____

☐ Payment enclosed (check or money order in U.S. funds)

Bill my: ☐ VISA   ☐ Mastercard   ☐ American Express   ☐ Discover

Card No. _____ Exp. Date_____ Security Code_____

Signature _____

MOUNTAIN PRESS PUBLISHING COMPANY
P.O. Box 2399 • Missoula, Montana 59806
406-728-1900 • fax 406-728-1635 • toll-free 800-234-5308
info@mtnpress.com • www.mountain-press.com

> *"Whether recalling wondrous Glacier Park adventures or getting primed for your first visit, this is one dandy book — beautiful photos and helpful info."*
>
> —GEORGE OSTROM, winner of a 2008 Telly Award for his DVD *The Seasons of Glacier* and author of three books on the park

GLACIER NATIONAL PARK
An A B C Adventure

KC Glastetter and Jeremie Hollman

There is a magical place where the grizzly bear is still king, mountain goats live among high craggy peaks, and glaciers dominate the horizon. From Avalanche Gorge to zigzag trail, ⌐ nature photographers KC Glastette⌐ Hollman take readers young and ⌐ by-letter journey through one of ⌐ treasures: Glacier National Park.

Children's Nonfiction/Nature/Travel

ISBN-13: 978-0-87842-552-5 $10.00
ISBN-10: 0-87842-552-7

51000

9 780878 425525

M MOUNTAIN PRESS PUBLISHING COMPANY

PQV104790